And the Stars Were Shining

AND
THE
STARS
WERE
SHINING

JOHN
ASHBERY

The Noonday Press
Farrar, Straus and Giroux
New York

Library of Congress Cataloging-in-Publication Data
Ashbery, John.
And the stars were shining / John Ashbery.
p. cm.
I. Title.
PS3501.S475A83   1994   811'.54—dc20   93-14255 CIP

*The author gratefully acknowledges the following publications in which
poems in* And the Stars Were Shining *first appeared:* American Poetry
Review, Chelsea, Colorado Review, Conjunctions, Forbes, Grand Street,
Harvard Review, Lingo, Mudfish, The New York Review of Books, The
New Yorker, PN Review, Partisan Review, Poetry *(Chicago),* The Poetry
Society, Princeton Library Chronicle, St. Mark's Newsletter, *and* The
Times Literary Supplement.

FOR ANNE DUNN

Contents

And the Stars Were Shining

TOKEN RESISTANCE

As one turns to one in a dream
smiling like a bell that has just
stopped tolling, holds out a book,
and speaks: "All the vulgarity

of time, from the Stone Age
to our present, with its noodle parlors
and token resistance, is as a life
to the life that is given you. Wear it,"

so must one descend from checkered heights
that are our friends, needlessly
rehearsing what we will say
as a common light bathes us,

a common fiction reverberates as we pass
to the celebration. Originally
we weren't going to leave home. But made bold
somehow by the rain we put our best foot forward.

Now it's years after that. It
isn't possible to be young anymore.
Yet the tree treats me like a brute friend;
my own shoes have scarred the walk I've taken.

SPRING CRIES

Our worst fears are realized.
Then a string of successes, or failures, follows.
She pleads with us to stay: "Stay,
just for a minute, can't you?"

We are expelled into the dust of our decisions.
Knowing it would be this way hasn't
made any of it easier to understand, or bear.
May is raving. Its recapitulations

exhaust the soil. Across the marsh
some bird misses its mark, walks back, sheepish, cheeping.
The isthmus is gilded white. People are returning
to the bight: adult swimmers, all of them.

THE MANDRILL ON THE TURNPIKE

It's an art, knowing who to put with what,
and then, while expectations drool, make off with the lodestar,
wrapped in a calico handkerchief, in your back pocket. All right,
who's got it? Don't look at *me*, I'm
waiting for my date, she's already fifteen minutes late.
Listen, wiseguy—but the next instant, traffic drowns us
like a field of hay.
                    Now it's no longer so important
about getting home, finishing the job—
see, the lodestar had a kind of impact
for you, but only if you knew about it. Otherwise,
not to worry, the clock strikes ten, the evening's off and running.

Then, while every thing and body are getting sorted out,
the—well, *you* know, what I call the subjunctive creeps back in,
sits up, begs for a vision,
or a cookie. Meanwhile where's the bird?
Probably laying eggs or performing some other natural function. Why,
am I my brother's keeper, my brother the spy?

You and Mrs. Molesworth know more than you're letting on.
"I came here from Clapham,
searching for a whitewashed cottage in which things were dear to me
many a summer. We had our first innocent
conversation here, Jack. Just don't lie to me—
I hate it when people lie to me. They
can do anything else to me, really. Well, anything
within reason, of course."

Why it was let for a song, and that seasons ago.

ABOUT TO MOVE

And the bellybuttons all danced around
and the ironing board ambled back to the starting gate
and meaningless violence flew helplessly overhead
which was too much for the stair
Better to get in bed they cry
since Zeus the evil one has fixed his beady eye on us
and will never come to help us

But out of that a red song grew
in waves overwhelming field and orchard
Do not go back it said for if there is one less of you
at the time of counting it will go bad with you
and even so, many hairy bodies got up and left

Now if there was one thing that could save the situation
it was the cow on its little swatch of land
I give my milk so that others will not dry up
it said and gladly offer my services to the forces of peace and niceness
but what really does grow under that tree

By now it had all become a question of saving face
Many at the party thought so
that these were just indifferent conditions
that had existed before in the past from time to time
so nobody got to find out about the king of hearts
said the woman glancing off her shovel The snow continued
to descend in rows this rubble that is like life infested with death
only do not go there the time should not be anymore

I have read many prophetic books and I can tell you
now to listen and endure

And first the goat arose and circled halfway around the ilex tree
and after that

several gazed from their windows
to observe the chaos harvesting itself
laying itself in neat rows before the circled wagons
and it was then that many left the painted cities
saying we can remember those colors it is enough
and we can go back tragically but what would be the point
and the laconic ones disappeared first
and the others backtracked and soon all was well enough

Today I would leave it just as it is.
The pocket comb—"dirty as a comb," the French say,
yet not so dirty, surely not in the spiritual sense
some intuit; the razor, lying at an angle
to the erect toothbrush, like an alligator stalking
a *bayadère;* the singular effect of all things
being themselves, that is, stark mad

with no apologies to the world or the ether,
and then the crumbling realization that a halt
has been called. That the stair treads
conspired in it. That the boiling oil
hunched above the rim of its vessel, and just sat there.
That there were no apologies to be made, ever
again, no alibis for the articles returned to the store,
just a standoff, placid, eternal. And one can admire
again the coatings of things, without prejudice
or innuendo, and the kernels be discreetly
disposed of—well, spat out. Such

objects as my endurance picks out
like a searchlight have gone the extra mile
too, like schoolchildren, and are seated now
in attentive rows, waiting trimly for these words to flood
distraught corners of silences. We collected
them after all for their unique
indifference to each other and to the circus
that houses us all, and for their collectibility—
that, and their tendency to fall apart.

THE LOVE SCENES

After ten years, my lamp
expired. At first I thought
there wasn't going to be any more this.
In the convenience store of spring

I met someone who knew someone I loved
by the dairy case. All ribbons parted
on a veil of musicks, wherein
unwitting orangutans gambled for socks,

and the tasseled enemy was routed.
Up in one corner a plaid puff of smoke
warned mere pleasures away. We
were getting on famously—like

"houses on fire," I believe the expression
is. At midterm I received permission
to go down to the city. There,
in shambles and not much else, my love

waited. It was all too blissful not
to take in, a grand purgatorial
romance of kittens in a basket.
And with that we are asked to be pure,

to wash our hands of stones and seashells—
my poster plastered everywhere.
When two people meet, the folds can fall
where they may. Leaves say it's OK.

JUST WHAT'S THERE

Haven't you arrived yet?
A sleepiness of doing dissolved my one
scruple: I lay on the concrete belvedere section
belabored by sun.
                        Nuts convened in the chancel,
a posse wheezed by in some oater: Chapter I, etc.

In the past I was bitten.
Now I believe.
Nothing is better than nothing at all.
Winter. Mice sleep peacefully in their dormers.

The old wagon gets through;
the parcel of contraband is noted:
a brace of ibex horns,
a scale worshipfully sung at the celesta.
We know nothing about anything.
The wind pours through us as through a bag
of horse chestnuts. Speak.

The orderly disappeared down the hall.
For a long time a sound of ferns rallied, then
nothing, only dumb snapshots of unknown corners
in strange cities. The tedious process
of fitting endings to stories.
Ground review. An obscurantist's trick.

Once you've wheedled as many as are there
at a given time, there's a certainty of dawn
in the not-much-else-colored sky. A phone booth
pivots daintily in air. O crawl back to the peach
ladder. A comic-book racetrack breathes somewhere.

A pianola was offered:
astonishment on the third floor.
The nice whore mended her ways.
The breathing came fast and thick.
The ushers will please take their seats.

TITLE SEARCH

Voices of Spring. Vienna Bonbons.
Morning Papers. Visiting Firemen. Mourning Polka.
Symphonie en ut dièse majeur. Fog-soaked Extremities.
Agrippa. Agrippine. Nelly and All. The Day
the Coast Came to Our House.

Hocus Focus. Unnatural Dreams. The Book of Five-Dollar Poems.
Oaks and Craters. Robert, a Rhapsody. Cecilia Valdés.
The Jewish Child. Mandarin Sorcerers. The Reader's Digest
Book of Posh Assignations. The Penguin Book of Thwarted Lovers.
The American Screwball Comedy.

Scenes of Clerical Life. Incan Overtures. The House on 42nd Street.
The Man in Between. The Man on the Box. The Motor Car.

Rue des Acacias. Elm Street and After.
The Little Red Church. The Hotel District.
I'll Eat a Mexican. The Heritage of Froth.
The Trojan Comedy. Water to the Fountain. Memoirs of a Hermit Crab.

The Ostrich Succession. Exit Pursued by a Turkey.
In the Pound. The Artist's Life. On the Beautiful Blue Danube.
Less Is Roar. The Bicyclist. The Father.

FREE NAIL POLISH

Cool enough. Granted,
she has beautiful legs, you know.
Men's thoughts are continually drawn behind
the apron of her success,
or to the tank top of her access
to the secrets of the great and philosophic,
of the most polite spirits
that invest these semitropic airs.

I need a tragic future to invest in.
Getting no support from others, I—
wait, here it comes along the rails,
a slow train from Podunk, the ironed faces
of the passengers at each window expressing something precise
but nothing in particular.

Yes, the mooing woods around this station are
partly extreme,
and wire fences are deep within
some parts of them. We know not
what they're for, nor why we snore
at a bug's trajectory
over the wallpaper's lilac lozenges.

TILL THE BUS STARTS

"This heart is useless. I must have another."
—*The Bride of Frankenstein*

I like napping in transit.
What I ought to do
just sits there. I like
summer—does it like me?
So much cursory wind
with things on its mind—
"No time to worry about it
now," it—she—says.

In short I like many
dividers of the days
that come near to eavesdrop on our thoughts.
What about gliders?
These, yes, I like these too.

And greened copper things
like things out of the thirties.
I must have one—no,
make that a dozen, all wrapped
fresh, at my address.

And were it but a foozle
schlepping round my ankles
by golly I'd give it the same
treatment all those guys,
years, gave me. You can't fasten
a suspender stud and not know about it,
how awful they looked,
and when they returned home under trees
nobody said
anything, nobody wanted it.

Still, I'll go
out in my way, waiting
for yet another vehicle.
It seems strange I read this page before, no,
this whole short story. And what
sirens sing to me now,
cover me with buttons?

Gracious exterior, but the rooms are small and mean
and so papered over with secrets that even their shape
is uncertain, but it is the shape of the past:
no love, no extra credit, not even civility
from those shades. Do they even see you?

They were so anxious for you to be there,
once, in the playground of what was happening to them.
Messages were bright then, hats undoffed,
manners fresh and cool, like a seasonable day
in early spring. The glancing
rivulets in the gutters struck a note that was a trifle flint-like,
though, and the birds were wary, warier than usual.

It took a man with a cane to magnetize
all those invisible and partly visible crosscurrents,
reluctant, downright sullen, or ones that hadn't yet had the time
to reflect on what was being set up here: a point,
no more nor less. Instead of trying to kiss you,
I too felt sucked into the ambient animal-revenge scene:
By twos and threes the animals returned, to their cages,
and sat obediently while the trainer barked orders at them.
They, it seemed, had nothing to lose. Nor in all the whitewashed domain
of the present past tense was anyone privy to the secrets
that now make us strong, or tall, and vulnerable
as a bride left waiting at the church, inching backward
to the cliff's edge as the photographer gets ready to smile.

THE STORY OF NEXT WEEK

Yes, but right reason dictates . . . Yes, but the wolf is at the door,
nor shall our finding be indexed.
Yes, but life is a circus, a passing show
wherein each may drop his reflection
and so contradict the purpose of a maelstrom:
the urge, the thrust.
And if what others do
finally seems good to you? Why,
the very civility that gilded it
is flaking. Passivity itself's a hurdle.

So, lost with the unclaimed lottery junk,
uninventoried, you are an heir to anything.
Brightness of purpose counts: Centesimal
victorious flunkeys seemed to grab its tail
yet it defied them with invention.
Stand up, and the rain
will be cold at first in your pockets.
Later, by chance, you'll discover supper
in the sparkling, empty tavern.
A nice, white bed awaits you;
your passport's in there too.

Acts have been cleaned up.
In the latest compromise
the hip audience mostly understands.
Unpleasantness, strange blips arise,
the nine-bathroom garage.
But where are we to begin again,
and what *are* we compared to Thee,
as two men scuffle in a checkout line
and a child bends
into the light, her knowledge of innocence
as a death now, name in the register
a gloved hand signs?

For what have we been rescued, if not
to see these and other things
that have no love for us?

For relishing something once done
in secret, and you lose footing further on,
out of the frame,

and everything that proves dimensionless is haggard.

He was something, wasn't he?
Until everyone has been let in and found sleep
we go his *way, profiting*
from the glances we get, the attentions to
special mores that are side-splitting.
And no caretaker comes to mulch us
once the ground is frozen,
no pike stabs the secret surface of earth
in time for a vigil of all you see.

The rose in the planetarium
asks for calm QUIET PLEASE can't you
see the door is leaking embers from that last, crucial light
we'd just stopped by for, like a mug of hot wine,
but it is soup that is being dashed in your face.
Then one day he sat down and wrote that line
that is so beautiful everybody wants to hum it
on this hillside, shoulders locked swaying to
its rhythm and the Master will come forward then,
the being no creation has seen,
perfect as a crowing cock in a ballad
most will have foretold, alas.
What wretch hasn't taught me that?

A WALTZ DREAM

She wasn't having one of her strange headaches tonight.
Whose fault is it? For a long time I thought it was mine,
blamed myself for every minor variation in the major upheaval.
Then . . .

It may have been the grass praying
for renewal, even though it meant their death,
the individual blades, and, as though psychic,
a white light hovered just above the lake's layer
like a photograph of ectoplasm.

Those are all fakes, aren't they?
In slow-moving traffic a man acts like he's going to be hit
by the stream of cars coming at him from both directions.
Like a cookie cutter, a steamroller lops the view off.

There are nine sisters, nine deafening knocks on the door,
nine busboys to be bussed—er, tipped. And in the thievery
of my own dreams I can see the square like a crystal,
the only imaginary thing we were meant to have,
now soiled, turned under
like a frayed shirt collar
a mother stitches for her son who's away at school,
mindful he may not care, may wear
another's scarlet and sulfur raiment
just so he take part in the academy fun.

And later, after the twister, slowly
we mixed drinks of the sort
that may be slopped only on script girls, like lemonade.
Who knows what the world's got up its sleeve
next brunch, as long as you will be a part of me and
        all what I am doing?

FALLS TO THE FLOOR,
COMES TO THE DOOR

That arrival, a foretaste of which appalls some,
assumed its rightful place as a statistic. "I don't suppose you . . ."
"No," I snapped, "nor at the opera, with the slush outside.
It seems to me a mildewed brick has been planted in my path
that wasn't there when I last looked . . . *but when was that?*
Why keep the charade up, if it matters so little,
like a tiny window or a bit of missing veneer?"
Then I get my hopes up.
So much gets sorted out in coming,
like the spring cleaning you always dreamed of.
What, me? It's as though an elf on a charger commanded
me to lie on my back, under the tree whose trunk
is swelling, becoming the world, it may be.
And I have galaxies to turn out, into the street,
in knickers, anywhere, so long as they be going . . .

One reads how another one's kinsman
has inherited a vast estate in Scotland.
The things that happen to other people! Surely
it was only a minute ago I caught you in a lapsed prayer
that was answered, you said it yourself. I, from this shelf
whence I see no land, not even space, can yet recall
how the ducks danced under their umbrella.
The past was peaches then.

THE LOUNGE

That it was a relief to him, my lord
who pestered me, with lint, with secrets,
always others' secrets, you knew
already. Two caitiffs were severed
from the trial, like a gordian knot.
That you knew too.

It is so hearty in this lounge.
Some bogus tint tampers
with the prairie sky in the mural,
makes it fresh, immediate, wrong
for these immaculate circumstances.

Then it's back to the old school, wagers,
brothels soon to come. It could have been settled
way back when so simply. But then there would have been no plot,
no peg to hang a dress on
of gauze the filmiest.

You, I suppose, wanted it this way
because we all want it this way.
Thus the story never gets sugar-coated,
protrudes like a bayonet from a shawl.

If there were others, they never came to see
what the disturbance was about. In fact there was
no disturbance, nothing to slide a hand along,
only postscripts and self-mutilation
the old way: cash and carry,
no refunds.

THE IMPROVEMENT

Is that where it happens?
Only yesterday when I came back, I had this
diaphanous disaffection for this room, for spaces,
for the whole sky and whatever lies beyond.
I felt the eggplant, then the rhubarb.
Nothing seems strong enough for
this life to manage, that sees beyond
into particles forming some kind of entity—
so we get dressed kindly, crazy at the moment.
A life of afterwords begins.

We never live long enough in our lives
to know what today is like.
Shards, smiling beaches,
abandon us somehow even as we converse with them.
And the leopard is transparent, like iced tea.

I wake up, my face pressed
in the dewy mess of a dream. It mattered,
because of the dream, and because dreams are by nature sad
even when there's a lot of exclaiming and beating
as there was in this one. I want the openness
of the dream turned inside out, exploded
into pieces of meaning by its own unasked questions,
beyond the calculations of heaven. Then the larkspur
would don its own disproportionate weight,
and trees return to the starting gate.
See, our lips bend.

is requested." That's where it began—
something like an engagement, with collusion
in its footsteps following. Like the slanted look
in the eyes of old portrait photographs—the three-quarters
view is more than sufficient to tell the ambition,
the dread.

There's some reality, too, some entertainment
here. Did you see where the couch rests
after dinner, the clearing up, the
white skirts around the house?
No one ever made it up but no one
made it sound better.

They dragged you out after that.
It wasn't until the leaves were partly rusted,
clashing with the fresh green, that a cover-up
was admitted. By then it was time to get new clothes,
new coals—to adjust. And some are still coping,

the mist still seems to cause them to blush
though it's only an illusion. After sex
there's nothing, only a reason,
a table of wearied books. A piece of lace
hung high up in the sky.

A HELD THING

Then he sort of lobbed it
over the fence if you know what I mean.

I do know what you mean
but I shall not tell anyone
about it until all your meaning
is clear to me, that is until it becomes clarity
that sucks us out of the void and across the orchard.
When I was a little teenager
I heard the far-off voices and imagined
them to be cries painted on a canvas.
Each had its own color, or a more vivid
approximation of that color, waiting
to be invited in for tea, or anything,
patted on the head.

I must haul myself down from there—
underbrush too thick with communion.
We've a million reasons for eccentric behavior
or even outright madness—you have only to choose one
and follow it to its logical conclusion.
Say you are sitting in that orchard,
mending or praying—the overhead rush
will make you think of a dog, and in time
wonder whatever happened to that dog.

Okay for starters but the colors
are more bleak and heavy now
but that's all right because more rounded,
human, like a statistic in mourning
for the body it used to represent
back in the good old days.

Now that you've come this far
it makes sense to take stock of you
in the mirror. Seams straight? "Seems"
they are. But you must get off the hood
of that car, or the bonnet, whatever the English call it,
for it to be happening, falling days and days
in dumb amaze. Happening like a city
of little explosions that protects
you wherever you go. And we need that protection—
It's colors, just like the ones were at the beginning.

STRANGE THINGS HAPPEN AT NIGHT

Without thinking too much about it,
prepare to go out into the city of your dreams.
Now, look up. At first they cannot see you.
Later, the adjustment will be made.
Your boyfriend sips bark tea.

The number should've turned up by now.
Perhaps the driving rain impedes it,
the recession. In any case there are two too many of us here.
We must double up, or die.

And that might be a practical if remote solution.
It's not every day you get to bicycle past the ribbons
of people, watch the grand hotels
for some event thought imminent—not lost.

If ever I was going to turn up your volume—
but this isn't about living, is it?
Or is it? I mean, many suppers in the seven modes
or grades, as many as can be made to last
once the bosses and their beagles have passed through.

WORLD'S END

Sometimes it's more time than we care to be,
with the others. Sometimes it's interesting.
I can only tell you how to stop things happening.

Life is legendary. We're very bullish
on life. Dogs and other lives
convince us life is dog-cheap.

The future is a ghost. The past,
it says here, is an automated manikin.
Not death, one of his plenipotentiaries.

Sea in my regards,
this life is lit
with all the sleep it can absorb.

I used to shuffle a lot. Someday
with luck, I'll make it to the newsstand
and buy some cherries, greet old friends.

ICE CREAM IN AMERICA

All of us getting our licks
and then some: the proud with the small,
those who fell off the canvas
and reappeared downstream.

. . . always forgets her pills, reverses herself, takes some.
The hen thinks chicks,
the man in the moon, profile: a piece
of the undoctored action.

We wake up, admire the day,
let our shoes take us where they will.
The weather's glorious:
a real shine.

Fill your cap with nuts.

Life in Japan is one of the most famous with all these
chairpeople and night stalls brewing
around a contradiction,
but the fowler knows his business takes him elsewhere,
telephoning, with more time to awake in the crystal pageant
of perplexed symmetries. Doomed because of it?
I never get hangovers until late afternoon
and then it's like a souvenir, an arrangement.
An old Dutch taxi takes us down to the sea
where other passengers are trying to change their reservations,
but the great flummoxed geodesic dome won't let them.

What will he do with it?
You're looking at an empire that has lost its clangor.
You get there by dying.

I tell particularly a thousand pounds of dust I saw
interspersed between the benign mountain-shapes
on the outskirts,
and how everyone was reasonably free to change. After all,
we make no effort to distinguish ourselves.
Those who wish to remain naked are coaxed out of laughter
with tea and nobody's nose is to the grindstone
anymore, I bet, and you can figure out these shivering trees.
But the owner of the bookstore knew that the flea was blown out of all
        proportion,
with September steps to go down in passing
before the tremendous dogs are unleashed.

LOCAL TIME

What can we do,
                    except
clasp, unclasp the hand that never is ours,
much as it wants to be? Under a gray skylight
the eclipse burns still, there are lilies, perfection
arrives, and then the tines
unearth fewer embers. Can it be time to go?

Models, when they undress,
misread the configuration even
while confessing to no version:
the heated or the clad. Tight boy,
you reminded me of dragonflies skulking,
of aromatic fires peaking,
and neither of us gets to know the other.
Next thing you know it's winter.
The skylight, now aproned with white,
is our bare harvest.

But there is good in reappearing:
the flames' roar, beaker of scotch, the old way
things were probably supposed to be all along anyway.

WELL, YES, ACTUALLY

To whom it may concern: Listen up.
About a year and a half ago a young man was in my office.
This young man,
whose name was Michael,
was the friend of another young man I already knew, Frederick by name.
Well, the upshot of it was, Michael,
who had pulled himself up by his bootstraps, wanted
to know the secret of things already not so secret,
like: Water, does it seem swollen, or how much does it weigh
when all the water molecules have been withdrawn,
and to whom does one address oneself after the correct answers have
     been passed around?
I told him, as best I could,
indeed, as I have told others in the past, that such soft
mechanisms, such software, can't be regulated, and if it could,
no one would want any answers. Well, he just sits there,
dumb. Then, as the call of the crow renews itself
across valleys and pastures, in the island at night,
the answer speaks in him too. Only it can't, he realizes right away,
ever be repeated. Or someone would pull nettles in exasperation,
slapping them all over the place, and then what devil-may-care
attitudes it pleases you to ration out will be flat as paper,
flatter than shadows peeled off of pavement. But I digress.

In this town, near this tree, a school rose proud and tall
once, and from a distance many were seen going in and out of it
as the bell sounded the hour from its red, hacienda-like tower.
And sure, mutts wandered in and out too,
and radish sellers. Well, one
man, a rustler to all appearances, wasn't happy
with the school and all its appurtenances: desks, faucets,
blackboard erasers and such. He thought it was a pity
that some come to learn and enjoy, while others plait
their tresses idly, in cool shadow, and read no book

and add no sum, the while the milk sours
happily, in the shade. And children from out of town would come
and look down at the others, and they too would fall to quarreling
until the teacher summons all, and says,
"Blessed children, my children. I would have it no other way
but this." And the man thinks, if that's what they teach you in school,
maybe I should go back to school. For I'm a loner, I warrant,
and loners never learn, though they may know the one thing
nobody else knows, or, by the same token, needs.
And a shadow fell across the fields
of radishes: This was the real, the genuine article,
and all other speculation had been slightly but sadly displaced.

And they thought about it. The teacher thinks about it to this day,
wondering where she went wrong,
why the prisms no longer irradiate electric colors
and the Bunsen burners cause no retorts to fume
and gurgle over, over the long desks that were.
These are the apples of my crying,
she says, the ones they never brought me, and I,
I am too distressed to dream.
Well, don't you think Michael and Frederick heard about it
and were the first to offer their condolences? But first
they swept all the chalk bits into a neat pile
and dedicated it to the stranger, and to the teacher they offered
the product of Pomona's blissful yearnings,
who dances alone all day by the sea, inebriated,
yet loves us as only a modern spirit can.
And they propped the door open
with a wedge-shaped piece of wood, so that it stayed open all the time.

MY GOLD CHAIN

Under the big Greenaway hat, the Diva,
diamonds aslant . . . Heavy trains hiss past, whiffing
the stench of Petersburg's canals, and the station
men's room thereof. What is it, spring? I can't

help being a little European. At times. After all.
I had no say in the matter.
He hollered at me later,
"Be gone, your phantasies, sun-dried hopes

simmered to a tisane of forgetfulness, forgetfulness
in May, when everything is beginning, or would be
if it weren't so shy. But check it out next week,
the meat that bleeds on newsprint

of the butchers' scales. But by then you may not need it,
in which case, why ask me? I'm only a doryman after all . . ."
Wind enters the slim curtains.
It was all right to be like this.

Nobody ever asked me to be a bridesmaid,
so maybe I'm a bride? The things you think of telling,
only you can't, you know, tell a leaf from a silver
chewing-gum wrapper. Things we mustn't know

but nothing we can't know. His song's over, I
better get ready to go on. Tell your readers
to write me, I love their questions, only it gets
so dark sometimes, you just want to stand and shake.

FOOTFALLS

O did he see something yesterday?
I cannot begin to say.

Something fell
on the floor.

A rice danger you have whipped up for us.
Congratulations, too, on the weather,
though I know you had nothing to do with that:
exhilarating, a bit flinty,
as a lock gets lost in a wash of wind.

When I've already stopped to do things, he
hasn't been able to insult you yet. Our love affair,
like dinnerware, lasted about a year,
then went away. My car's still in the rut,
but who could have foretold these greennesses,
the girl with the aigrette
who didn't barely want to sleep there?
But when we all came out, the day
assumed the role of host, did what was necessary.
Above the architecture were
tinseled outcroppings, a space in between.
In short it was marvelous, the young master was mad to have us,
but until such time as the thorny legal angles
can be worked out, joy must stay
imprisoned in the air around us, like humidity.

Today there were no tassels.
Funny, I'd gotten used to them,
and to the bells on your toes.
There's a story in that,
she said. I'll tell you later.
Two have already been supportive.

WEATHER AND TURTLES

The rain fell with startling regularity.
Sections of understanding were imposed
on the lake—a likable but needy reservoir—
and on that great instrument, the street.

Okay, but can we have a little luster,
here, please, a little texture? It's like a weekly occurrence,
this laughing at the limbs of people
who march by you, intent on shopping
or seeing the world—whatever, so long
as it has nothing to do with you, frantic dimwit
on your nightmarish carousel of doubt, who sees
and yet proclaims, and sees on, but no one
can stop the demented *danse macabre*
ensuing from soda fountains, shoestores, penny arcades
buried in a stratum of light like cheese.

It's the old dumb-show thing now.
I see, I read, I nap.
Thankfully the chimaera never came near me,
relaxing in its cave.

SOMETIMES IN PLACES

And patient, exacting
no confirmations from those who know him,
the poet lies down under the vast sky,
dreaming of the sea. For poetry, he
now realizes, is cleverer than he.

So where to go, what to be in?
For as the robin builds a nest,
so each day weaves a bower of itself
to offer to the world. I am standing
here listening, but no one word proves the truth,
though several do. And we shall acclimate
towns, cities, sunsets, to our desire, O
accidental mandarin, and the purple
velvet of plenty dominate
our dreams, for a while, and then we shall
nod to the post, and be off again.

Day falls of its own weight.
And basing your luck on that,
you too enter the skirmish
of ghosts and dragons, and so are blessed
with deafness to the clamor of surviving
frogs' catcalls. Forgot your lunch,
was it? No, I thought you had one.
No, that was mine.

WILLIAM BYRD

With the precision of one who fights, slowly, the shadow of the battering ram of absolute knowledge behind him, in a barrel-vaulted, hallowed space . . .

The gnomes' contumely notwithstanding, it was a red-letter day, really for all concerned, and then the tide poured in. It is fatal to forget this nugget of charm even as one flounders knee-deep in it, smashing at gulls, cries, the wind . . .

Art-deco priestesses summon from distinct alcoves brains made for discerning timekeeping ordeals. The little pennants that flutter ominously from the rigging of ships cannot help but evoke a charred red entity, staircase landing for some. Blue is the cobalt at which we point our belts, energetically, soulfully.

Tied in some neurosis competition, I was happy to see you as a little girl at your birthday party so many years ago, changed, and with a glove for each tear-starred hour of the day. It was graceful then to be back-bending, to half-turn as the obsessed host comes into one's line of vision, from a nameless spree, polite and indifferent, most indifferent to his politeness and that of others. For we live in a three-channeled creekbed and there are no balloon-offenses leaving from here.

I thought you had drilled the dendrite of your extra keeping into my forehead by now, flesh the texture of a reed.

And you know, the skunk family approved it too, including old Grandpa skunk. But which does not take us very far from wars and their canons. The chipped, dried paint managed to signal enthusiasm. There was beginning to be in the world like a low cloud of birds circling. The higher you direct our gaze the less it sees the struggle at your feet, out of which a victor will emerge, and yes the orphans play with us often on the sand until one by one they get adopted. Which is why the angles are all acute ones and it's colder than the inside of a pocketbook.

Suddenly, shambling
she comes up to me, a thing partly of architecture,
of how it would like to be the basis for *all* partaking,
communicating, and is in arrears because of some
dumb thing over your head. Oh well. The misery of others
is a sad thing to behold but one must contemplate as well the gathering
that goes on, in bits, in pits, whatever is exposed at low tide.
The brief diamond that you dangled . . . And then all want to come to
        see, tremendous
crowds overwhelm the dock, which threatens to collapse under their
        weight, but
they want to see, they *get* to see. At first it's like some
phenomenon's unbirthing, then a cold star, but always an alphabet
        among whose
letters are interlaced much affection and dying.

Hold my stinger as a stranger and I will be presently.
I haven't filled out the forms.
I can see heaths and coasts;
in them we become magic and empty again.

ASSERTIVENESS TRAINING

I like the integrity of what you have to say,
drama or dream. What is credibility
without assertiveness, endurance without skepticism?
And the abrupt thrust of your bearing
at me under a low-hanging branch.
What shall any of these do without skeletons
as ideas? I hear the tango beginning,
the waltz that is loss. Crossed logs in the chimney . . .

Without aggressiveness, hope, I couldn't conquer any of it.
There'd be no piece of it to bring back to you,
saying, "This is me." A lie
among others we're exposed to. And when the needle finally swung
it was wrapped in rags, in pitch blackness.
I escaped from the dream of living
into a fairy tale with no happy ending, no ending at all,
only bedtime to live ever after.

You could climb a fence amid barberries
and never see the departing smile on the swan's face.
Only your need will be redeemed
when you dwell again among us, much misunderstood.
For now your glass prayer encases both of us.

LIKE A SENTENCE

How little we know,
and when we know it!

It was prettily said that "No man
hath an abundance of cows on the plain, nor shards
in his cupboard." Wait! I think I know who said that! It was . . .

Never mind, dears, the afternoon
will fold you up, along with preoccupations
that now seem so important, until only a child
running around on a unicycle occupies center stage.
Then what will you make of walls? And I fear you
will have to come up with something,

be it a terraced gambit above the sea
or gossip overheard in the marketplace.
For you see, it becomes you to be chastened:
for the old to envy the young,
and for youth to fear not getting older,
where the paths through the elms, the carnivals, begin.

And it was said of Gyges that his ring
attracted those who saw him not,
just as those who wandered through him were aware
only of a certain stillness, such as precedes an earache,
while lumberjacks in headbands came down to see what all the fuss
    was about,
whether it was something they could be part of
sans affront to self-esteem.
And those temple hyenas who had seen enough,
nostrils aflare, fur backing up in the breeze,
were no place you could count on,
having taken a proverbial powder
as rifle butts received another notch.

I, meanwhile . . . I was going to say I had squandered spring
when summer came along and took it from me
like a terrier a lady has asked one to hold for a moment
while she adjusts her stocking in the mirror of a weighing machine.
But here it is winter, and wrong
to speak of other seasons as though they exist.
Time has only an agenda
in the wallet at his back, while we
who think we know where we are going unfazed
end up in brilliant woods, nourished more than we can know
by the unexpectedness of ice and stars
and crackling tears. We'll just have to make a go of it,
a run for it. And should the smell of baking cookies appease
one or the other of the olfactory senses, climb down
into this wagonload of prisoners.

The meter will be screamingly clear then,
the rhythms unbounced, for though we came
to life as to a school, we must leave it without graduating
even as an ominous wind puffs out the sails
of proud feluccas who don't know where they're headed,
only that a motion is etched there, shaking to be free.

TWO PIECES

I

Edith and Julian
waiting, awaited by others
in the hills, yes.

But by what unobstructed parade
ground do I reach that hill?
For it is
        simple to say
the coordinates when they greet you,
not like getting on with life,
not the street.

II

When the cauldron is
tipped, whatever
is in it flows outward
like the mouth of a river
taking out its dentures.

No obit, more socks.
And a stray whoosis
that knew your name once
now sits on the floor.
Now no aftershocks.
The horse's mane tears—

THE FRIENDLY CITY

Unless you put it away
he can never play with it again,
the marimba, and you know what that means.

Our city bemoans us, or does it
only seem to? Showers that come in shifts,
light poles guarded in air,
the dry cackle of trees in the Botanical Gardens?

Was it for this suburban marketplace
you wrote, and are writing still
in that wire-bound notebook?
Things like: "Man cannot stand what he has become
but he loves to lap up his own vomit"?

In that case the city will probably stay around
for most of the day. It likes your sleeping sound,
not the bad silence of the others
who are even now clogging its approaches,
giving the place a bad name.

Oh if it was a name he wanted
why didn't somebody say something?
We could have found him one so easily
like "Elector of Brandenburg,"
and the city could have seen its reflection
finally, a ducal palace, upended.

THE DESPERATE HOURS

The man, someone's uncle, went down
to where the barrier said to him why
do you disturb a corner of the universe
that is yours that had been yours
before either of us was invented?

He said truly I did not know I snore.
He said truly I invented a hoof medication.

But these are tangible, lazy things—
what about the uncertain, pallid ones
they gave you at birth to play with?
Why did not the city centers
come to be called what is this town?

He said I never saw any but chaste cheeks reflected
in her armor. The tower leans
O more desperately than it has done
these twenty centuries past.
Why is it my dungheap, my rosary?

And in this true saying all are warehoused,
the flatirons, the jib, even the two horses
not paying any real attention.

But it is your watch fob,
your crenellated bow window, bent
indeed like a bow, that's why they call them that,
your small town, your farm of about forty acres
outside it. Your wart. Your five-year diary.
Your intention to have made this once it had passed.

THE DECLINE OF THE WEST

O Oswald, O Spengler, this is very sad to find!
My attic, my children
ignore me for the violet-banded sky.
There are no clean platters in the cupboard
and the milkman's horse tiptoes by, as though
afraid to wake us.

What! Our culture in its dotage!
Yet this very poem refutes it,
springing up out of the collective unconscious
like a weasel through a grating.
I could point to other extremities, both on land
and at sea, where the waves will gnash your stark theories
like a person eating a peanut. Say, though,
that we are not exceptional,
that, like the curve of a breast above a bodice,
our parabolas seek and find the light, returning
from not too far away. Ditto the hours
we've squandered: daisies, coins of light.

In the end he hammered out
what it was not wanted we should know.
For that we should be grateful,
and for that patch of a red ridinghood
caught in brambles against the snow.

His book, I saw it somewhere and I bought it.
I never read it for it seemed too long.
His theory though, I fought it
though it spritzes my song,
and now the skateboard stops
impeccably. We are where we exchanged
positions. O who could taste the crust of this love?

THE ARCHIPELAGO

Well, folks, and how
about a run for the sister islands?
You can see them from where you stand—
will you barter vision for the sinking feeling
of lumps of clay?
          The daffodils
were out in force, as were, improbably, the nasturtiums,
which come along much later, as a rule. But so help me,
there they were.
          She said, may I offer you some?
His tangling so flummoxed him,
all he said was "Boats along the way."

Really, there are so many kinds of everything
it halts you when you think about it,
which is all the time, really—oh, not *consciously*,
that would be a waste, but in sly corners,
like a rabbit sitting up straight, waiting for what?
We can study drawing and arithmetic, and the signs
are still far away, like a painted sign
fading on the side of a building. Oh, there is so much to know.
If only we weren't old-fashioned, and could swallow
one word like a pill, and it would branch out thoughtfully
to all the other words, like the sun following behind the cloud shadow
on a hummock, and our basket would be full,
too ripe for the undoing, yet too spare for sleep,
and the temperature would be exactly right.

Miserere! Instead I am browsed on by endless students,
clumps of them, receding to this horizon and the next one—
all the islands have felt it,

have had their rest disturbed by the knocking knees of foals,
by kites' shrieking. And to think I could have had it

for the undoing of it,

                          snug in the tree house, my plans
open to the world's casual inspection, like an unzipped fly—
but tell us, you must have had more experiences than that?

Oh the cross-hatched rain, fanning out from my crow's-feet,
the angry sea that always calms down,
the argument that ended in a smile.
These are tracks that lovers' feet fit.
But at the end they flag you down.

GUMMED REINFORCEMENTS

Insane, trapped together in a . . .
How would you like one?
Growing up is what it is,
leaning into the wind, without a cent.

We had the most beautiful childhood
and lunch—that's even better.
I only paid $4.75 for mine.
An embarrassment, considering
it would be an embarrassment for me too.

Then he frolicked and said, whatever happens
happens in a dream,
eleven, twelve, fifteen times a day.
Sometimes when you are away
it happens at night,
all night.

Children we had lost once
know how to keep repeating the piece
they learned, knew the way back to us,
us, as grave robbers, of an old candy store
with a cake as centerpiece: a wild,
fragile one. Therefore read this:
a sun, mild as any, with diamond-tipped consequences
somewhere. An atmosphere of brooding, perhaps . . .

Yes! And the cake was square!
How did you guess? And all along, a
stork was creeping up the stair
to its bower, injured by the furniture
and last-minute preparations. Nobody
came to sign its register.
There was no one in the large drum

a canker folded over, looking
at you real mean-like.

And I and the dream are still only acquaintances
after all this time, a century, it seems,
from Arkansas. Did the goats get milked in time
for your hand to graze it? Was the squall over then?

Those who paint the heavenly porch
put a damper on all our ideas, extreme creations
like love. You heard me, ladies—
past and pure truth, swaying,
light out over the land.

The crowd of robbers doesn't go away.
It would rather be sunset, if that were inexorable
enough. But it's not. Count the pigeons, the people,
townspeople, running fast in all directions.
Sign here for the blanket of furze, please.

I must proceed unflustered.
I should have shopped around.
After all, comparison shopping is what this place's
all about. I think. These are very crisp.

Nothing like a big stranger in the dark
"to concentrate the mind," as Dr. Johnson said.
Venetian blinds are for keeping close watch on—
there goes another one!

And if there is no peace in declarations
they may become ornaments. After all, superstitions
did once, and aren't they very like history,
even the same thing as?

Back then when someone said "Pigs in a blanket,"
these shifting animals in nordic drapery
would coalesce. Today, other pieces of statuary
from far and near, near and far,

are hastening toward the whirlpool of history.
Well, let them try it. And if a few old pros
want it, let them try it too. Let this frangible
passing moment be the last to know, as usual.

WHAT DO YOU CALL IT WHEN

The fire betokened it
as a woman means many things
in this deck—
that's why unsavory characters

He knew that out of hiding
the fire would burn fast at last
providing the smooth yet crinkled edge
so much flatness requires

that from savannas
the kitchen landscape may begin:
amazed quinces
the drink on the corner
so everything would be a red or a blue sign

Crowders-out of old age
assassins of youth
gentlemen walking:
the trustees of this enterprise.

It is not difficult to single out one pearl in a bushel of them. What's needed is to set us back on the track, having gently peed, and that for some orpheum other than ourselves. Some shelter that is not us.

They laughed and began to dance in a ring, heads bobbing, ankles sweeping, the same old private dance that is remorse for not having blossomed sooner and the poison of this day, under vines, to correct that stance.

Fairs and cupolas notwithstanding it is a tray of cameos to be brushed past, the invisible seizure, as when crowds don't find what they are looking for.

So I came at last to you for the comedy of it, and in this I have no regrets, only silences, secrets, and the mask that was sent me long ago. I repeat it in paragraphs in these parts and am not ready to go home yet.

PLEASURE BOATS

Wash it again
and yet again.
The equation drifts.

Wallowing in penguins,
she was wallowing in penguins.

With fiendish cleverness
the foreground closes in.

The four-leaf clover loses.

PRETTY QUESTIONS

The two parks interfaced,
of summer earth,
of shroud and color,
red hope.

Are you growing up to write your novel now?
He'd been waiting on tables for several years,
lost without a stinger.
Should travel agents travel less?
The girls can never be free of the volcanoes' might.

Anybody not having any?
See, it was like tar between the boards,
outlines, though without force or purpose—
just things to drag
along, carry along, to meet a fee
with. And the damage
during the minute was requested:
that it was over last night
before quitting was necessary,
in a certain way that I was going to tell you about.

They came at me with ice-cream implements.
You read it first here.

Why you are all blue,
your shoes are too,
so is the barrel of space that encloses us.
Maybe everything is.
We should want it to be.
Help. I have to go to the bathroom.
Why, there's your difference, of course,
your having to come down
from the park, gorse-scented,

and the pleasing treetops.
Not much of this was ever mine
but some of it had to be for
me to invest it with a shine.
Go on. I'll go on doing that
if we can stay together, play together.

The two mountains *were* all mine.
They are yours now.
That is, you can have them if you want them
and the day that comes with them.

PATHLESS WANDERINGS

Whereas I, efficacious ruin,
in former times a ladder, no quarter
gave to the bullies as they were emptying out
of school, in the time of roses.
It seems I grew exceeding tall.
There was something wrong with most men.

Women, however, were overcome with sympathy
where the last lawn tennis had been.
In my sleep I shared tears and bread
with my loving companions. We were three,
stamped with the bravura of those times.

I can tell you not one swatch matters now.
The tide has come in once too often.
We kneel to say our prayers
to an enormous kettledrum. The reeds' stance
perfects the searchlight's curving grasp,
sleeps behind things.

Which is what we all . . .
Then when I saw the ball descending
and felt the air crisped for the packaging of me
I did what others before you have done:
appeared to you as a raven in a dream
that washed away all landscapes, now and to come.

Too bad the birds don't like their bath.
I like it cheaper,
and to have the exact change,
teeth for this meat.

ON FIRST LISTENING

TO SCHREKER'S *Der Schatzgräber*

The woman with the confused soul keeps calling.
Was gibt es? Now that you're in Honolulu you've got to live it up
no matter what kind of grub they throw at you
on Main Street. O but my past is operatic
you see, the glitter, wink and shimmer,
all are in my bones. The hegemony of irrational
behavior always leaves the by-then-very-determined hoplites astonished,
they moan in groves. Or do you prefer

the sea? How about this empty, gravel-encrusted courtyard?
The sea please. A time of increased understanding.
Such things as male bonding didn't exist.
En revanche, ponytails were something small horses wore.
Asses in gear, we frisked in salt-air sunlight. Obviously a whole lot
aren't going to exist today; we should be thankful for it
and pick up our rooms, for tonight the night will be bright,
fewer of us than can stand it will be chosen,
examined, tossed cruelly into corners like rag dolls
missing one or more limbs. Say, then,
what did you want when you came here?
Was it to subvert our cunning, our lust,
and turn them back on us, reflections in a chipped pocket mirror?
And if so why then utilize us
as indicators? Our auras are unsafe,
or so we think, so we have been taught. And those who graze them
invariably come to grief.

But that's just what life's about, isn't it?
So your coming sped our just deserts.
One is off with a nerd in a pothole somewhere.

And we can have, have, I say,
whatever surplus barriers come our way.
But be brief. What remains to be quizzed will be spelled out for us
in the epilogue, in the unheated crawl space under the eaves.
The time of the fool approaches. And an aureole is running.

DINOSAUR COUNTRY

So, with a bath and tin words,
the stranger settled in. Just so,
the evening idlers—lorikeets, back-
scratcher vendors, declined to take cognizance.

Everyone waits for the BIG day
that happened billions of years ago
or is definitely tomorrow—take your pick—
while fending off tunnel vision in the race
for the sauna. The new purple bath towels
are here!

But what if on a subtle
sky-ridden day some scum comes up to you and sez:
"Jeez! Can't anybody take a joke anymore?
I was only asking after the missus and those ten
dear, dim orphans whistled for the fur to fly.
Now I'm on an island in a self-engrossed river
with the selected essays of Addison and Steele
and enough K rations to last till Michaelmas
and its daisies, which, incidentally,
bloom only for me."

I'd thought no one knew about the pact between me and Junior.
But a woman getting off a bus twisted her ankle and shouted:
"For the last time! My dwelling place is no longer your oven
no matter how much you fancy its delicately frosted petits fours."

And then there was the time
when you just joked coming
up to me, laid your wrist on
my shoulder and whispered the news about
the Romans: They'd won again,
and, what was more to the point, done so

in an era that surpassed the age of the dinosaurs
by as much as this minute moment of pleasure
scoffs at you for the taking, and you flash your sweatshirt
for everyone in the country to see, and hold on to.
Yes, there are shadows still, but
cheap compared to the price you'd pay for not gainsaying
that sail swooping toward you, for not getting even
with the white-haired acrobats.

LEEWARD

Up, up it rises,
the penumbra,
for all to see.

Heaven is open—
make no mistake.
That row of books
just slid over by itself,
and a guy, a tubby guy,
came to look at it, sneer,
snicker, be off again—only,
ouch! There are other strands
in that equation, he sees now, not
too late. The green spoilage,
all other things being equal,
may be contained.

Only wear your shirt right.
Wash it again
and yet again.
The bear is still around
whose hide you sold,
wondering why children fear him.
Is it too much to ask
safe conduct, yes, for him too
in the travesty of night
we all must wear
for a while?

PARAPH

I have to sign my name
to this paragraph. Writing pieces you can't use up
till the bus starts. I feel like a beer,
buxom brew.

One felt secure, reading
the edge of a newspaper.
More schools come out. An overload.
Destiny and the comics. Two can't play
as one. In the box outside
the golf course hasn't disappeared.

Spot watering of test areas
guarantees a mediocre result. We can dance
to it.

We can't read around the edge, the rim
is whiter before we were done.
Check this out. A situation
in which no situations appear.

And the code is locked in your throat.
We should be leaving or
the bird will chide us,
no chime break.

NOT PLANNING A TRIP BACK

And the ignorance on your hands is August,
is white August. Breathe but on a stone
and a common wish-fulfillment is put in reverse.
All these dinners you paid too much for—
not worth writing about? Then the astral walk
resumes. Men are playthings. I've been
notified before.

Or pause before a bush in August,
and the trepidation that is natural in men
takes root here too, is bigger than before
but not so just. Take a boat ride.

I give to strangers—make that, I grieve to strangers,
asking no rebuttal, no rebuke. The jackass
is off his rocker again. How pliant the gold of the stars
is! We stare and stay, then part anyway.
There's a reason for this, but it's shut up
in a tomb, somewhere.

Oh the wind whips through here sometimes.
Gosh, does it? Can't these feuds
ever be removed, like lace panties?
Can't we stare down the stair
that's coming to get us? If we had the right look
everything could be secular, and easy.
But the soul isn't engaged in trade.
It's woven of sleep and the weather
of sleep. Forgets what there is to hide.

MYRTLE

How funny your name would be
if you could follow it back to where
the first person thought of saying it,
naming himself that, or maybe
some other persons thought of it
and named that person. It would
be like following a river to its source,
which would be impossible. Rivers have no source.
They just automatically appear at a place
where they get wider, and soon a real
river comes along, with fish and debris,
regal as you please, and someone
has already given it a name: St. Benno
(saints are popular for this purpose) or, or
some other name, the name of his
long-lost girlfriend, who comes
at long last to impersonate that river,
on a stage, her voice clanking
like its bed, her clothing of sand
and pasted paper, a piece of real technology,
while all along she is thinking, I can
do what I want to do. But I want to stay here.

MAN IN LUREX

It's only a matter of days now.
The luster on the child's eye says so.
Be back before morning she says.
O return! Return so that my enemies may see me
lolling in the grape arbor.

Once we've given our brother a breather
where is the hill that will take us down?
He loved the formal: sonatas and knot gardens
and more manner than one had anticipated:
alienating, idled.

Down farther: the economics of doubt,
this carapace, gives pause to some.
For us it is the very concept, the scent
of home. As snowshoes are meant for snow.

IN THE MEANTIME, DARLING

The time is for going out
and across.
One woke up and wished he was dead.

There is for everyone a solemn feeling
unless you put it away.
Go on adumbrating he said.

Go on listening because
eavesdropping is the only way to write.
O so you're doing a handbook again.

Thought I'd ankle over.
Then the sea rushed past.
Hurricane Charlie and his sister
sure were glad to see us.

At times there is a daze
with a diamond-like purity.
These and others could be sent for later.

It's not the food in his mouth.
He'd hear others could become
and just drift away.

Pterodactyls still haunt
the ethnic ballpark.
It's better this way,
just inside this window
as night approaches.

JUST FOR STARTERS

Charges about this unhappiness:
They would run out and stay a minute,
exhibit the requisite stinginess,
roll up in a blanket.

That's how they and she looked to you and me.
But of course we were vendors of a sort,
tied to no actual drift, and so
when it became poorer and spoons were put up for sale
we stood in our back alleys, chagrin
painted brilliantly on our faces.

I don't know what got me to write this poem
or any other (I mean, why does one write?),
unless you spoke to me in my dream
and I replied to your waking
and the affair of sleeping and waking began.

No matter how hard I try
I can't get back on the tricycle.
Look, a fish is coming to save us.
A sail nods gallantly in our direction.
Maybe unimportance isn't such a bad thing after all.

BROMELIADS

In my original philosophy for the age of gink
it felt like a harp was being plucked.
How not to respond to those suggestions, if that's what they are,
like little breezes lifting grass and leaves,
as a delta of mattering fans out from
a point like a minimal encounter.

That's how I faced up and got far away
from the lucky island and arrived at this place of crossings
where no two things occupy the same outline
in both space and time. It's as if the people
who brought you up were to abandon you in your best interests
so as to bring on a crisis of enlightenment—
and then jump up from behind furniture and out of closets
screaming, "Surprise! Surprise!" But it's not clear
just who ages in the process. I look ever closer
into the mirror, into the poured grain of its surface, until another I
seems to have turned brusquely to face me, ready
to reply at last to those questions put long ago . . .

Will we achieve anything? Not likely.
But as starlings occur in patterns, and in pairs, it
seems that *does* mean something and you shouldn't stay
in your cave until this century is forgotten.
Who'd pay the photographer then?
Did I tell you your prints are ready,
that you look as reckless as an enchanter emeritus
and weary as the first gables of spring?

COMMERCIAL BREAK

Take care of values. The rest is shopping,
raiding the islands
for what little coral they possess.

Tell me . . . You opted for the shrimp cocktail.
I have no more
sand in my shoes. The witch squints at the fire.

SICILIAN BIRD

The perfume climbs into my tree.
It is given to red-haired sprites:
words that music expresses
almost amply.
     The symphony at the station
then, and all over people trying to hear it
and others trying to get away. A "trying"
situation, perhaps, yet no one is worse off than before.

Horses slog through dirt—hell,
it's normal for 'em.

And that summer cottage we rented once—remember
how the bugs came in through the screens, and
all was not as it was supposed to be?
Nowadays people have cars for things like that,
to carry them away, I mean,
I suppose.
     And wherever man sets his giant foot
petals spring up, and artificial torsos,
dressmaker's dummies. And an ancient photograph
and an ancient phonograph, that carols

in mist. Pardon. The landlord locked us out.

MUTT AND JEFF

> "But what he does, the river,
> Nobody knows."
> —HÖLDERLIN, *"The Ister"*

Actually the intent of
the polish remained well after
the soup was nailed down. Remnants to cherish:
the sunset tie old Mrs. Lessing gave me,
a fragment of someone's snowball.

And you see, things work for me,
kind of, though there's always more to be done.
But man has known that ever since the days
of the Nile. We get exported
and must scrabble around for a while
in some dusty square, until
a poster fragment reveals the intended clue.
We must leave at once for Wabash.

And sure enough, by the train side the blue-
uniformed bicycle messenger kept up easily
and handed me the parcel.
"Ere the days of his pilgrimage vanish,"
I must reflect on exactly what it was he did:
how lithe his arm was, and how he faded
in a coppice the moment the yarn was done.

Still, the goldfish bowl remains
after all these years like an image
reflected on water. It was not a bad thing
to have done what I have done,
though I can imagine better ones, but still
it amounted to more than anyone ever thought
it would. The mouse eyes me admiringly
from behind his chair; the one or two cats
pass gravely over or under my leg from time to time.

The point is there's no bitterness,
not here, nor behind the scenes.

My sudden fruiting into the war
is like a dream now, a dream palace
written for children and others, ogres.
She was braining my boss.
The day bounced green off its boards.
There's nothing to return, really:
Gumballs rattled in the dispenser, I saw
my chance for a siesta and took it
as bluebottles kept a respectful distance.

COVENTRY

There was one who was put out of his house
and another that played by a pond
of a lateness growing,

one that scalded his hand.

And now, he said, please deny there was ever a house.
But there was one and you were my mirror in it.
These lines almost convey the comfort of it,
how all things fitted together in their way.
But it was funny and we left it—
her address, her red dress.

Just stay out in the country a lot.
You have no house. The trees stand tentless,
the marmoreal floors sweating . . .
A delusion too.

Good thing. Good luck.
You'd have to stay in Coventry.
But I'm already there, I protested.
Besides, doesn't any leaf or train want me
for what I'll have stopped doing when I'm there,
truly there? Yet who am I to keep anything,
any person waiting? So we diverged
as we approached the city.

My way was along straight boulevards
that became avenues, with barrels of trash burning
at each corner. The sky was dark but the blue light in it
kept my courage up, until the watch spring
broke. Someone had wound it too tight, you see.
Then I could only giggle at the odd bricks,

corners of tenements, buildings to be leased.
I fainted, honey.

And I never saw you again
except once walking fast
across the Victorian station
lit by holiday flares
yet strangely dumb and rumorless
like all the sleep and games that jammed us here.

AND THE STARS WERE SHINING

I

It was the solstice, and it was jumping on you like a friendly dog.
The stars were still out in the field,
and the child prostitutes plied their trade,
the only happy ones, having learned how unhappiness sticks
and will not risk being traded in for a song or a balloon.
Christmas decorations were getting crumpled in offices
by staffers slumped at their video terminals,
and dismay articulated otherness in orphan asylums
where the coffee percolates eternally, and God is not light
but God, as mysterious to Himself as we are to Him.

Say that on some other day garlands disbanded
in the fresh feel of some sea air,
that curious gulls coasted from great distances
to make sure nothing was getting more than its share
of pebbles, and the leaky faucet suddenly stopped dripping:
It was day, after all. One of those things like a length of sleep
like a woman's stocking, that you lay flat
and it becomes a unit of your life and—this is where it
gets complicated—of so many others' lives as well
that there is no point in trying to make out, even less read,
the superimposed scripts in which the changes of the decades
were rung, endlessly, like invading kelp, and
whatever it takes to be a simp is likely not what saved you
in time to get here, changing buses twice, and after,
when they sent you to your corner to lick
your wounds you found you liked licking
so much you added it to your repertory of insane gestures,
confident that sleep would punish those outside
even as it rescued you from the puzzle of the dance,
some old fire, thought extinguished, that now

blazes in the stove, and in an instant we realize we are free
to go and return indefinitely. Is that

what you meant by lasting? Oh, sure,
hedgerows are in it too, and the doves there and insects
and treed raccoons that eye one with frank disapproval:
"You unmitigated disaster, you!" I was pleased to discover
one could flatten or otherwise compress it, its Tom
Tiddler's ground having induced only a subcoma, a place
where grown men drink screwdrivers and giggle at the melee
that would certainly have resulted if someone, some prince regent or
        sheriff,
hadn't been in charge, while the long day moped
and opened the fan of its grievances, harassment
being the only one that stands out in the blur now, after such distance.

The steed returned home alone, requiting all previous loves.

II

To have been robbed of a downturn
today, I have drunk some water,
rollicked in the texture of a late,
unfinished sonata,
sinking into snow,
falling forward in the oratory,
violent as the wolf's cue and anything
you take from that side of the ledger
only beware of boredom, boredom-as-spell.

Then, slipping into the gentle jacket of
my having to know why everybody passes me,
how I cursed that heir, braided that subway
of signals seen only from behind,
the old rug and its mug—all were madness for me,
yet only dust. And as I undid its much-stitched
frogs, a near melancholy approached
from across the lake—little slivers
of sense unbent, that were right about it all
in their way, though I unlatched these tears,
bleached for the occasion.
                            The stairs knew
it was under them, but by the same token couldn't acknowledge
the enormous debt lifted from the mountain's brow.

And the same foreman, the same teacups jingle still,
following a localized pattern,
uncovering what till now has been everyone's pill.

III

The nude thing was taken around
to various ambassadorial residences.

And on the day he had come home
to see her, her in the maze of
sandwiches some artisan proposed,
he was like a bee in summer.

Remember the reflexive mode, the soul
can live with that, or live behind
it he said, to no avail. The last
breasts caught up.

And in morning like sugar she gave her head
to the toll-places the mind suggests.

I V

divide the answer among them
on the façade of the spinning jenny as it
approaches improbably,
a toxic avenger . . .

Later amid the hay of reasons
we sort out a sparse claim.
Was it to be thirty he dressed her
in black-and-white checkers of gingham,

or,

perforce, did the lad go athirst
thinking no doubt too late of the spines,
pelage of mingled hairs and spines,
when all would have meant protection
for him from the main highway, the chief.

A porch

rattles in the near, clear distance.
There was never any insistence on a name,
though we all have one. Funny, isn't it?
Yours is Guy. I like "Guy," "Fanny" too,
and they grow up and have problems same as us—
kind of puts us out into the middle of the golf course
of the universe, where not too much ever happens,

except growing up, hook by hook,
year after tethered year.
And in the basement, that book,
just another thing to fear.

V

The problem
would have to have had so many other things wrong with it
to remain remonstrably a problem that we would have had to float,
it to its bottle of capers, I to my mound of gin,
for the others to see us and pretend not to notice.

That would have been the bonanza, the great volcano,
but as they say in Cheyenne, "Ain't some weekends no
more than sister days of the week when it comes to volleyball
and dimity shrouds," and aquarelles are for the masses
to live off of, when food and conversation run out.
I know because I was a kid with a banana,
but that's for eternity only. All other gaps open out
in the mind of the possessed. I'll be glad to

repeat what I said in court, but send
no lawyers after me, no *papier bleu*, if you please . . .
And the spider shinnied down the thread it was making as it did so,
curious about what other alarming event could be occupying this same
        moment,
and when he got there, well, it was too late. Death
makes no excuses and, by the same token, exacts none.
The race
is to the fit, and it's a great day for the race,
the human race, yes, but also the tent race,
and my husband is as a cored apple to me:
beautiful, sometimes, and in and out of the dark.

We cared less for each other
than any two people on earth, but the point is we cared.
Don't tell the scotties we didn't.
They wouldn't believe you anyway—it's just
that my mind is full of eyes, days like this.

VI

A silly place to have landed,
I think, but we are here.
The door to the dressing room is ajar.
A tremendous fight is going on in there.
Later, they'll ask and you'll say you heard nothing
out of the ordinary, now, not that day.
Madame had gone out . . .

So bring the scenery with you.
Midwife to gargoyles, as if all or something
were appropriate, you circle the time inside you,
plant an asterisk next to a kiss,
and it was going to be okay again, and the love
of which much was made settles closer, is a paw
against a wrist. Hasn't finished yet,

though the bread-and-butter machine continues to churn out
faxes, each grisette has something different
about her forehead, is as a poinsettia
in the breeze of Rockefeller Center. I don't like
a glacier telling me to hurry up, the ride down is precipitous.
Then a smile broke out on the ocean face:
We had arrived in time for the late lunch.
The dogs were instructed not to devour us.
And so much that in the past
was kept in flavors of ice-cream sodas now jumps
into one's path. We'll have to
take note of that for tonight's return trip,
though silver sleighbells pamper us,
hint that we'll get to see the Snow Queen
after all, at long last, obscuring the fact
that somebody *was* running along the courtyard.

Then the janitor wasn't screwy, the mickey
he was to have been slipped was stuck in heavy traffic,
and all those conversations about carbon dioxide
were a smokescreen too. How brittle it all was,
in the way abstractions have, and yet how
much it mattered for those children: It was their
funeral, and they should have had a say in its undoing
by the lighthouse's repeated lunges.
He claimed it was to read Sir Walter Scott by.

No one ever questions *him*. That asparagus-like mien
wasn't made to encourage dolts and stutterers.
Yet I think a clue is back here
behind the sofa, where lost bunnies whimper
and press together. He *had* been a seafarer,
who knew where his last hamburger
had come from, and whose cursive signature adorned
the polished bullet. In a little while peace
would establish itself, welcome foreigners and venture capital,
and tides rush in to destroy
what little progress in unleashing the sense of things
I and my classmates had made. We were still
at the beginning of the alphabet, chanting things like "Tomes
will open to disgorge intuiting of our altered dates,
we stepchildren, who had no place to go, and nowhere
to be late, and brash breezes
play with our buoys. Still, a little consideration
might have helped, at that point." And time will be as precise
as a small table with a cordless telephone on it, next to a television.

V I I

Rummaging through some old poems
for ideas—surely I must have had some
once? Some people have an idea a day,
others millions, still others are condemned
to spend their life inside an idea, like a
bubble chamber. And these are probably
the suspicious ones. Anyway, in poems
are no ideas. No ideas in things, either—
her name is Wichita.

Later with candles coming to the
celebration, it occurred to me how
all this helps—if it wasn't here
we'd be like lifeguards looking for prey.
Look, one of them stops me. "Your
candle, sir?" Dammit, I know there was something
I was supposed to remember, and now I'm lost.
"Oh no you're not, the smile on that big
bird's beak should be enough to let you in
on the secret, and more." He's here to help,
the whole darn nation is, even as
tidal waves suck at its precipices and high-speed
dust storms dement its populace. One
will say he's seen an anchor in the sky—
why am I telling you this? It's just that the light,
violet, impacted, made a difference
for a moment
back there.

The bug-black German
heels and back areas, the long tilted
cloaks for sale, the others—yes,

they're still here?
Something must be done about it
before it does it itself. You know
what that will be like. The white tables with their
roses are so beautiful. It doesn't matter if the corn is faded.

VIII

I've never really done this before.
See, I couldn't do it. Does this
make a difference to you, my soul's
windshield wiper? See, I can try again.

Now, try to expose it.
We'll look back and it won't seem
so long ago. This late in Dec.
you go from day to night in 32 minutes,
the peonies ajar—

That which I polished
as a child stands up to me.
A peashooter blows away
the soldiers.

I have seldom encountered more libidinousness
on the road to the tracks. My shanty
looks okay to me now, I can live with it
if not in it,
who had the prescience—the prescience of mind
to buy a part of New York
while it was still a logo on someone's umbrella,
a rococo convict from the Laocoön tableau.
Those snakes get worse each season
the deaf man said
and he had reason
on his side, they were strangling his kid
and goat even as we talked in the parched
weather that was obscurely damp and white.
Next swamp we'll do better,
tidy up things, the davenport

that got thrown out, the kerosene lamp
you wanted for your henhouse. The stoves,
so many of them. The refrigerator:
Eskimos really do need them
to keep their food from freezing
you said to the teacher, and my eye
is dry, all the riddles come undone.

Hot, swift choices
over the lake in May.
The old gray mare.
Violets blossomed loudly
like a swear word in an empty tank.
The fish mostly had gone home
the admiral repeated falling into
his habitual stammer—whenever he came
to the words "iron blow" it happened for him,
poor rich man, who despised the stall tickets
once he recovered from the rage
of being within us again.

And whether it was smoke on a balcony
or idle laurels that seem to creep
out of his books in the library
we were chastened—"by the experience"
and so went to bed and never read again.
It was glorious standing up in the various rain
to keep clear of the teeth but that changed nothing
fast like a fast game of checkers.
The kind of cry that can't be heard

yet others outside might know of
soon as the mist was sucked
up through a tube and the platonic curve

returned for various dignitaries to perch on
like members of the Foreign Legion or the French Academy.
Androgynous truths never shattered anyone's
complacency on Broadway even though they use thermal down
now (I thought it had been outlawed)—
beckoning though maybe not at you
as you come to evaluate
all the leaning together.

And the store models are free
for the asking—aye, that's just it,
"for the asking." What isn't? And who
can make that chirp
sound round in the eye of the traveling salesman—
taller than might have been expected, than Mont Blanc—
who sees the talisman perishing amid lichees
while others gape and walk back toward
Washington Square.

If I had night I would feed it to you
but I have something much better—the desire to run
away for president, with you
in my back seat. And whether butter
brings a smell of gas with it or the Beefeaters
look bloated, all is of some concern to us—
we didn't need to be separated before you knit that
sweater as a plenary indulgence: shimmering
with only pastel colors like a life lived
near sunlight exclusively, like a page turner's
romance with the page and the soloist.

It breaks into thunder:
thought that comes to you,
a safe haven from the shipping.

Lo, a low hill welcomes those who wish
to climb its flanks, to its summit
just over the near horizon, blue and cream,
the colors of my navy she said, I'll bet yours
are similar too. That was why I had to play
my gray cape, the lost card

no one is ever conscious of having.
And if we had something for the stew,
some salt or something, why that could go in too
as long as land could still be sighted
to the left, a silver crow's nest in which all
lost objects, blue Christmas tree ornaments, arise
and sing the national anthem of Hungary
and the river garments come together with a clap
to shield those who never previously wore them
and the gold tooth extracted from a brooch
join in the general clamor
of do-gooders—the common sort of folk
all over us like a coat of burrs.

Once the bear knew he headed back to his cave.

Winter wasn't clear yet
but all the days of the year were tumbling out of its crevices,
the chic ones and the special-interest ones,
and those with no name upon them.
Everything looked slight
which was all right.

Then the magician entered his chamber.
Too bad there are no more willows
but we'll satisfy his bent commands anyway,
have a party in the dark,

throw love away, go neck in the park,
fill out each form in sextuplicate—then let the storm
be not far behind, the old graves and swords
of winter erupt out of turn. It won't be bad
for us. You see, the penguins have stayed away too long,
ditto the flamingos. I think I can make it all
come together, but for that
there must be a modicum of silence.
Your ear's just the place for it.

IX

New technology approaches the bridge.
The weir, ah the weir, combing the falls,
like the beautiful white hair of a princess.

In the oxidation tank he thinks
of fish, how strange they can get the oxygen
they need from the water, and then when it goes blank—
why, pouf! And you realized the past suffered
from housemaid's knee, and that when the present
came along, why no one would speak up,
and it just moved in, with pets . . .
For the medium future I had thought striped stockings
and a kind of beard like a haze, seen only
on certain ancient sun deities who walked
absorbed in fields, as children groused
and crocuses sputtered the unbelievable word.

Right, it's definitely our situation.
We can come out of it but not simply leave it.
It will die of having so many things in it,
like a barrel choked with leaves. Yet sooner or later,
you know, one is dipped in it
and spotted lawns, greatcoats emerge.
The cistern really was built
by the workmen while you were away.
It's alive and containing.
And so many horticulturalists sway,
inebriated with the hardiness
of the ranunculus, the gladiolus.
Even so, he asked us to leave him
alone, at night, wanted to think

or something, about love or something,
something that turned him on.

Only later when we came to bask
in his friendship, did that marine eye astonish us:
Out over so much plains, such doo-wop wind,
you'd think it wouldn't spell "ceremonial" to him.
But he merely shaved the numbers off, dawn removed
the fingerprints, and why I am with you
and these several elves, no one can piece together:
not Great-aunt Josephine or her mortician boyfriend,
not the robbers of the "School of Night" drawing.
And we shifted, you and I, causing the rowboat to take on water.
Strange, how a few decibels can make your day.

X

Of course some of us were more risible—then.
Stopping by an apartmentful of freeloaders
on a snowy evening, I was asked about the *other*
mysteries, and, forced to prevaricate, noted
that time was setting in.

As one gets peeled away from life
and distant waterspouts put their kibosh on the horizon,
just one message makes it through the triple filters:
Go easy. Your chums on this shore have
worked long and hard on the inclined-plane thing;
if you haven't any suggestions (and you haven't),
let them continue to think it was sorcery
that was lacking. The fact that no directional
arrows pointed the way to the mother lode
proves their greenery to them, and they begin
to reason: "The kitchen's not such a bad place,
if it's sinks you're after. Sure, Caruso was singing
somewhere behind the padlocked velvet door,
but if we stay—no, linger—here, the problem
will reverse itself. Tom and Jerrys all around."

As for the ritual endowment
so prized by the Coca-Cola girl, that only arrived later
to prove its wetness and wildness non-fatal
just before the sun came out and caked it.

We sure live in a bizarre and furious
galaxy, but now it's up to us to make it
into an environment for maps to sidle up to,
as trustingly as leeches. Heck, put *us*
on the map, while you're at it.
That way we can smoke a cigarette, and stay and sway,
shooting the breeze with night and her swift promontories.

XI

"But in the soul of man there are innumerable infinities."
—THOMAS TRAHERNE

There is still another thing I have to do.
I've never *been able to do this*
and I have this announcement to make
over all the streets, all the years we have been difficult
leading to this. This icon. That walks and jabbers
fortuitously or not. Bells splinter the ice
and I am away, on a trip somewhere. Kansas.
It doesn't matter for me
and matters so old for you, sobs distant as tractors.
We are the people we came to see
or might as well be, bringing cabbages as gifts,
talking nonstop, barbed wire stringing the trees,
cigar smoke bellowing.

It was all the same to us,
we came in and out,
were thoughtful as strawberries, and the great athlete overturned us,
made us obsolete. Now that was a day I can trace
with a little mental calisthenics
and find I know what I was doing, to whom
I spoke, the kings, carriages, it was all there.
And my knowing derives no comfort
from that parallel shelving of events.
No kind of nexus. As if the doll herself knew
what you weren't supposed to know, and survived the fall
from the attic window to incriminate you,
just before the draft swept her into the furnace.
The burning is beginning again.

But there are a giant two of us,
the remnant, or product, or a complex
bristling-up-around, then a feigning of disinterest
in a corner of the room, and the fuse ignites
the furniture with blue. It's earth-shattering, they say,
as long as you contain it,
and you have to, can. The brain-alarm is being recalled
but the message exists even with no words to inflict it,
no stanzas to be cherished. For we end
as we are forgiven, with chords the bird promised
caught in our throats, O sweetest song,
color of berries, that I lied for and extended
improbably a little distance from the given grave.

XII

A late glimmer read into it
what is not to be intuited,
only pressed, like a hand or pants,
as the sea presses against rock
for lack of anything better
to do—surrounded by buddies
taking a breather, it was always thus with you,
you who come close enough to me:
Oh, you've often found
clues in the garden where the hornets
and the robins make their nests;
clues on the stairway, in the vestry
and the garage with its enormous drums.
Say something that will strengthen me,
let me sip all the colas of the world
before I dive off this reef, into
that region of ferns and bubbles that awaits us,
where all are not so bright, but a few are.
These we clasp to us, our bodies' tattoos
seeking psychiatric help, and the earth
guzzles and slurps rhythmically.
A dog would like you for it,
but here no voice says to come all the way in.

Here are holdings,
taking name in the urban dusk
that grazed you just now. Have you brought the lesson?
Good, I was sure of it. But can no longer
go out past the doorman. Here, take this basket of iced cookies
anyway. And he jubilates. Everything is in time for him,
eating in the capacity, along with the French
and motorcycle community, is what the headphones told us.

And when we no longer have each other to look at
these buzz and resonate still. From what dark pitcher
or mirror I brought you, from Duluth, and minus
astral influences, you are grateful, and for wrappings in general.
It is time to feast
so soon again.

Slow crows still rally round that puncture mark
in a Danish heaven where a sawhorse delivers
the belated aspirin and spools are wound
in the interests of a greater clarity than this:
Soon, all will be hidden,
like a stage behind a red velvet curtain,
and this mole on your shoulder—no need to ask
it its name. In the brisk concealment
that has become general everything thrives:
bushes, lampposts, motels at the edge of airports
whose blue lights guide the descending vehicle
to a safe berth in soon-to-be night,
as wharves welcome their vessels, however frumpy
they may seem, with open arms.
And I think it says a lot about us, about
our welcoming, that days don't disturb themselves
or think too much about it, or manage
the disheveled trace that was to have been our signature.
We're too cagey for that in any case,
wouldn't be fooled by the most elaborately duplicated passport,
bill of lading. It's as though we've come refreshed
from another planet, and spied immediately what was lacking in this
        one:
an orange, fresh linens, ink, a pen.

Still, the hothouse beckons.
I've told you before how afraid this makes me,

but I think we can handle it together,
and this is as good a place as any
to unseal my last surprise: you, as you go,
diffident, indifferent, but with the sky for an awning
for as many days as it pleases it to cover you.
That's what I meant by "get a handle," and as I say it,
both surface and subtext subside quintessentially
and the dead-letter office dissolves in the blue acquiescence of spring.

XIII

You get hungry,
you eat hot.
Home's a cold delivery destination.
The emphatic nose puts it on hold.
Clubs are full.
I kind of like the all-night dust-up
though I'm sworn to secrecy,
with or without a cat.

I let so many people go by me
I sort of long for one of them, any
one, to turn back toward me,
forget these tears. As children we played at being grownups.
Now there's trouble brewing on the horizon.

So—if you want to come with me,
or just pull at my sleeve, let them make that discovery.
Summer won't end in your lap,
nor are the stars more casual than usual.
Peace, quiet, a dictionary—it was so important,
yet at the end nobody had any time for any of it.
It was as if all of it had never happened,
my shoelaces were untied, and—am I forgetting anything?